GOOD MORNING, GOD! I SEE YOU!

CYNDI CRAFT

"Arise, shine, for your light has come,
and the glory of the Lord has risen upon you."

Isaiah 60:1

Palmetto Publishing Group
Charleston, SC

Good Morning, God! I See You!
Copyright © 2020 by Cyndi Craft
All rights reserved

First Edition

Printed in the United States

ISBN-13: 978-1-64111-956-6
ISBN-10: 1-64111-956-X

Special dedication to:
William H. "Bill" Craft
Best Dad a girl could ever ask for.
I miss you every single day!

And

Mrs. Rebecca Dunn
Hands down the BEST English teacher to ever grace the classrooms of
Whitehouse High School and a faithful servant of Christ her entire life.
Thank you for all you gave!!!

ACKNOWLEDGEMENTS

To Melissa S., thank you for the encouragement to do this book! To Kristy F., Brian K., and Cherie J. – your unconditional love, acceptance and friendships are irreplaceable and appreciated more than words can say. Much love to you all!
Cyndi

THE LORD'S PRAYER

Our Father who art in heaven, Hallowed be thy name
Thy kingdom come, thy will be done,
On Earth as it is in Heaven.
Give us this day our daily bread and forgive us our trespasses as
we forgive those who trespass against us.
Lead us not into temptation but deliver us from evil.
For thine is the kingdom, the power and the glory for ever and ever.
Amen

Introduction

Hi, everybody! Having doubts about whether God knows you're there? He does. Wondering if He cares about what you're going through? He does. Think He's forgotten you? He hasn't. Questioning His plan for your life? We all do!

We all go through our own hills and valleys – times of darkness, times of sunshine and favor. During one of my especially dark times – quite possibly the worst – I found great peace drinking coffee on the front porch. The house itself was one of the worst I've ever lived in, but it kept my kids and I safe and the porch faced the East. I spent many mornings sitting there listening to and watching night turn into day. It became my "God time." Every morning as the sun peaked over the horizon, I said out loud, "Good morning, God! I see you!" This became a tradition that carried over to the car when I finally found work again. On one particular morning leaving the high school after dropping off my kids, the idea to post this morning tradition to Facebook flittered into my head. I laughed at myself and decided I might be losing it. A few hours later, I made the post.

The response astounded and humbled me. After a few months of doing this, a friend suggested I make these posts into a book. The rest is history.

The purpose of this book is to shift your perspective and change your focus from your burdens to your blessings; to the One who loves you most. There are no rules - open it anywhere and give it a go. Remember, Jesus meets us where we are. He is all inclusive, not standards-related exclusive. My hope is that you find peace and assurance through establishing or improving your relationship with the God of your understanding. The lined pages are for your thoughts, blessings, fears….get it out and give it all to God. Write down where you see God that day. It's far too easy to get caught up in our problems, disappointments and failures. We must remember to focus on the blessings.

Good morning, God! I see you!

CROWDER - "RED LETTERS"

"…My dead heart began to beat
Breath of God Filled my lungs
And the Holy Ghost awakened me…"

"But by the grace of God I am what I am, and His grace to me
was not without effect."
I Corinthians 15:10

Good morning, God! I see you!

THE EDWIN HAWKINS SINGERS - "OH HAPPY DAY"

"O happy day…When Jesus washed…our sins away…"

"Do not seek revenge or bear a grudge against one of your people, but love your neighbor as yourself. I am the Lord."
Leviticus 19:18

Good morning, God! I see you!

PASSION – "IN CHRIST ALONE"

"…No power of hell, no scheme of man,
Can ever pluck me from his hand…"

"Above all else, guard your heart, for everything you do flows
from it."
Proverbs 4:23-27

Good morning, God! I see you!

NEWSBOYS – "HE REIGNS"

"…And all the powers of darkness
Tremble at what they've just heard
'Cause all the powers of darkness
Can't drown out a single word…"

"I am the bread of life. He who comes to me will never go hungry, and he who believes in me will never be thirsty."
John 6:35

Good morning, God! I see you!

MATTHEW WEST – "HELLO, MY NAME IS"

"…These are the voices,
These are the lies
And I have believed them
For the very last time…"

"Do not let your hearts be troubled, trust in God, trust also in me."
John 14:1

Good morning, God! I see you!

NINA SIMONE – "FEELING GOOD"
"…Oh freedom is mine
And I know how I feel…"

I have told you these things, so that in me you may have peace.
In this world, you will have trouble. But take heart! I have
overcome the world!"
John 16:33

Good morning, God! I see you!

BETHANY DILLON –
"HOLY IS THE LORD"

"We stand and lift up our hands
For the joy of the Lord is our strength…"

"For God so loved the world that he gave his one and only Son,
that whoever believes in him shall not perish but have eternal life."
John 3:16

Good morning, God! I see you!

COREY ASBURY – "RECKLESS LOVE"

"When I was Your foe, still Your love fought for me
You have been so, so good to me
When I felt no worth, You paid it all for me
You have been so, so kind to me"

"For I know the plans I have for you, declares the Lord, plans
to prosper you and not to harm you, plans to give you hope and
a future."
Jeremiah 29:11

Good morning, God! I see you!

SIDEWALK PROPHETS – "LIVE LIKE THAT"

"I want to show the world the love You gave for me
I'm longing for the world to know the glory of the King"

"Trust in the Lord with all your heart and lean not on your own
understanding. In all your ways acknowledge him,
And he will make your paths straight."
Proverbs 3:5-6

Good morning, God! I see you!

LAUREN DAIGEL – "O LORD"

"Oh, O'Lord O'Lord I know You hear my cry
Your love is lifting me above all the lies
No matter what I face this I know in time
You'll take all that is wrong and make it right…"

"I can do everything through Him who gives me strength."
Philippians 4:13

Good morning, God! I see you!

ZACH WILLIAMS – "RESCUE STORY"

"…There you were in the shadows
Holding out Your hand You met me there…"

"Ask and it will be given to you; seek and you will find; knock
and the door will be opened to you."
Matthew 7:7

Good morning God! I see You!

HILLSONG UNITED – "GOOD GRACE"
"…Fix your eyes on this one truth
God is madly in love with you…"

"Jesus said to her, 'I am the resurrection and the life. He who believes in me will live, even though he dies; and whoever lives and believes in me will never die."
John 11:25-26

Good morning, God! I see you!

HILLSONG UNITED -
"OCEANS (WHERE FEET MAY FAIL)"

"Your grace abounds in deepest waters
Your sovereign hand
Will be my guide
Where feet may fail and fear surrounds me
You've never failed and You won't start now"

"Then He arose and rebuked the wind, and said to the sea,
'Peace, be still!' And the wind ceased and there was a great calm."
Mark 4:39

GOD, GRANT ME THE

Serenity

TO ACCEPT THE THINGS I

CANNOT CHANGE...

Courage TO

CHANGE THE THINGS I CAN

AND *Wisdom* TO

KNOW THE DIFFERENCE

Good morning, God! I see you!

MATT REDMAN – "10,000 REASONS"
"Bless the Lord oh my soul
Oh my soul
Worship His Holy name
Sing like never before
Oh my soul
I'll worship Your Holy name"

"Peter replied, 'Repent and be baptized every one of you, in the name of Jesus Christ for the forgiveness of your sins, and you will receive the gift of the Holy Spirit."
Acts 2:38

Good morning, God! I see you!

BIG DADDY WEAVE – "REDEEMED"

"…All my life I have been called unworthy
Named by the voice of my shame and regret
But when I hear You whisper, 'Child lift up your head'
I remember oh God, You're not done with me yet…"

"Do not judge, or you too will be judged. For the same way you judge others, you will be judged, and with the measure you use, it will be measured to you."
Matthew 7:1-2

Good morning, God! I see you!

PHILLIPS, CRAIG & DEAN –
"REVELATION SONG"

"Clothed in rainbows of living color
Flashes of lightning, rolls of thunder
Blessing and honor, strength and glory
And power be to You the only wise King, yeah"

"Behold, I am coming soon! Blessed is he who keeps the
prophecy in this book."
Revelation 22:7

Good morning, God! I see you!

HILLSONG UNITED –
"PRINCE OF PEACE"

"Your love surrounds me when my thoughts wage war
When night screams terror, there Your voice will roar
Come death or shadow, God I know Your peace will meet me
there…"

"The God of peace will soon crush Satan under your feet. The
grace of our Lord be with you."
Romans 16:20

Good morning, God! I see you!

MERCYME - "BEST NEWS EVER"

"Some say, 'don't ask for help'
God helps the ones who help themselves
Press on, get it right
Otherwise, get left behind
Some say, 'He's keeping score'
So try hard, then try a little more
Hold up, if this were true
Explain to me what the cross is for…"

"Therefore, do not worry about tomorrow for tomorrow will worry about itself."
Matthew 6:34

Good morning, God! I see you!

FOR KING AND COUNTRY
– "BURN THE SHIPS"

"So long the shame, walk through the sorrow
Out of the fire into tomorrow
So flush the pills, face the fear
Feel the wave disappear
We're comin' clear, we're born again
Our hopeful lungs can breathe again
Oh, we can breathe again…"

God, I offer myself to Thee – to build with me and do with me as Thou wilt. Relieve me of the bondage of self, that I may better do Thy will. Take away my difficulties, that victory over them may bear witness to those I would help of Thy Power, Thy Love, and Thy Way of Life.
3rd Step Prayer – Alcoholics Anonymous

Good morning, God! I see you!

MERCYME – "GRACE GOT YOU"

"So when you're standing in the rain again
You might as well be dancing
Why? 'Cause there ain't no storm that can change how this ends
So next time you feel blue
Don't let that smile leave you
Why? 'Cause you have every reason just to.."

"'Come, follow me,' Jesus said, 'I will make you fishers of men.'"
Matthew 4:19

Good morning, God! I see you!

CASTING CROWNS – "ONLY JESUS"

"All the kingdoms built, all the trophies won
Will crumble into dust when it's said and done
'Cause all that really mattered
Did I live the truth to the ones I love?
Was my life the proof that there is only One
Whose name will last forever?"

"This is how God showed his love among us; He sent his one and only Son into the world that we might live through him."
I John 4:9

Good morning, God! I see you!

DOWNHERE – "HOW MANY KINGS"

"How many kings step down from their thrones?
How many lords have abandoned their homes?
How many greats have become the least for me?
And how many gods have poured out their hearts
To romance a world that is torn all apart?
How many fathers gave up their sons for me?"

"Oh Lord almighty blessed is the man who trusts you."
Psalms 84:12

Good morning, God! I see you!

LAUREN DAIGLE – "TRUST IN YOU"
"When You don't move the mountains
I'm needing You to move
When You don't part the waters
I wish I could walk through
When You don't give the answers
As I cry out to You
I will trust, I will trust, I will trust in You."

"When I am afraid, I will trust in you. In God, whose word I
praise, in God I trust; I will not be afraid."
Psalms 56:3-4

Good morning, God! I see you!

DC TALK – "WHAT IF I STUMBLE?"

"Father please forgive me for I can not compose

The fear that lives within me

Or the rate at which it grows

If struggle has a purpose

On the narrow road You've carved

Why do I dread my trespasses will leave a deadly scar?"

"Suppose one of you has a hundred sheep and loses one of them. Doesn't he leave the ninety-nine in the open country and go after the lost sheep until he finds it?"

Luke 15:4

Good morning, God! I see you!

LAUREN DAIGLE – "FIRST"

"Before I speak a word
Let me hear Your voice
And in the midst of pain
Let me feel Your joy…"

"No one can serve two masters. Either he will hate the one and love the other, or he will be devoted to one and despise the other. You cannot serve both God and money."
Matthew 6:24

Good morning, God! I see you!

THE AFTERS – "WELL DONE"

"What will it be like when my pain is gone
And all the worries of this world just fade away?
What will it be like when You call my name
And that moment when I see You face to face?"

"His master replies, 'Well done, good and faithful servant! You have been faithful with a few things and I will put you in charge of many things. Come and share your master's happiness!'"
Matthew 25:21

Good morning, God! I see you!

BETHEL MUSIC –
"RAISE A HALLELUJAH"

"I'm gonna sing, in the middle of the storm
Louder and louder, you're gonna hear my praises roar
Up from the ashes, hope will arise
Death is defeated, the King is alive!"

"Love the Lord your God with all your heart and with all your
soul and with all your strength."
Deuteronomy 6:5

Good morning, God! I see you!

RAY STEVENS – "EVERYTHING IS BEAUTIFUL"

"Everything is beautiful in its own way
Like a starry summer night or snow covered winter's day
Everybody's beautiful in their own way
Under God's Heaven, the world's gonna find a way…"

"Stop judging by mere appearances, make a right judgement."
John 7:24

Good morning, God! I see you!

CHRIS TOMLIN – "I WILL RISE"

"And I will rise when He calls my name
No more sorrow, no more pain
I will rise on eagles' wings
Before my God fall on my knees…"

"Be strong and courageous, do not be afraid or terrified because of them, for the Lord your God goes with you, he will never leave you nor forsake you."
Deuteronomy 31:6

63

Good morning, God! I see you!

TAUREN WELLS – "KNOWN"

"It's so like You to keep pursuing
It's so like me to go astray, ooh
But You guard my heart with Your truth
The kind of love that's bullet proof
And I surrender to Your kindness, oh…"

"But when you give to the needy, do not let your left hand
know what your right hand is doing, so that your giving may
be in secret. Then your Father, who sees what is done in secret,
will reward you."
Matthew 6:3-4

65

A SIMPLE PRAYER

Lord, make me an instrument of Your peace;
Where there is hatred, let me sow love;
Where there is injury, pardon;
Where there is doubt, faith;
Where there is despair, hope
Where there is darkness, light;
Where there is sadness, joy.

O Divine Master, grant that I may not so much seek to be
consoled as to console,
To be understood as to understand, to be loved as to love.
For it is in giving that we receive,
It is in pardoning that we are pardoned,
And it is in dying that we are born to eternal life.
~Amen

St. Francis of Assisi